Proofreading by Alexander Christian Logan & Chloe Rebecca Logan

ISBN-13: 979-8-9956811-3-7

Cover design by: JMLocusol (The last known location of the painting used in the cover design was at a church in Harrisonburg, Virginia.)

Contents

Introduction

How can we Pray ?

Floods, Fires, Earthquakes, Storms, Plagues. We are aware of all of these around us. Do we pray for each person who has COVID, each person who has lost someone to malaria, each person suffering from an earthquake? Or everyone who lost their livelihood, everyone suffering from disease, and every family who has lost a home in a Hurricane? Or even displaced by war and starved by injustices? In a world where a list of prayers is seemingly endless, one must ask: Where do we start?

Sometimes, even knowing how to pray can feel desperate.

Pondering this reminded me of how Jesus taught his followers to pray.

Start by acknowledging God, "hallowed be." Followed by a request for hope for all the Earth. "Your Kingdom come, your will be done, on earth as it is in heaven."

I pause here and see hope… Would Jesus teach his followers to ask for something unattainable ? If we are to think of heaven as a wonderful place, instilled with Peace and Justice, surely we are guided to ask for the same on earth. It must be possible then, right ?

Ask for the basics: "Give us today our daily bread." Interestingly, we are not asking for tomorrow's meal.

Forgive our mistakes, for yes, we all make them. "Forgive us our debts, as we forgive our debtors." It is implied that we are to forgive others as well.

Protect us from evil. There is no denying that evil surrounds us, and we require protection from it. "Deliver us from evil."

Then we end with Praise for God, "the kingdom, the power, and the glory are yours now and forever."

I find solace in following simple, prayerful steps: Acknowledge God. Ask for good for all. Ask for your basic needs. Ask for forgiveness. Remember to forgive. Request protection from the evil we encounter. End with thankfulness that God is Great.

What is written in these pages is not written with any authority, simply thoughts that I felt I should share. Prayers can be their own songs, art, or photography. These have helped me at least, and so I hope it may help others as well.

Prayers

Morning Prayer

Creator of all, you are amazing!

May this world we live in be as you intended, a place of Peace Justice, and Love for all.

Feed us today.

Forgive us for how we have harmed others.

Help us to forgive, and protect us from the evil around us.

For this is your creation,

You are all-powerful and amazing, today and for eternity.

Prayer before meal

Thank you Jesus for this day and for your love,
and thank you for the food.

Prayer before Bed

Thank you Jesus for this day and for your love,
and help us to sleep good tonight.

Prayer for times of distress

(repeat as often as needed)

Lord God Creator of All, Please help!

Lord God Creator of All, Please help!

Lord God Creator of All, Please help!

Lord God Creator of All, Please help!

Lord God Creator of All, Please help!

Lord God Creator of All, Please help!

Lord God Creator of All, Please help!

Prayer of Justice Light & Love

Creator of all, Architect of life.

Where is your justice when human justice is pushed aside?

Where is your compassion when human compassion is pushed aside?

Where is your power when human power prioritizes itself over all else?

Where is your anger when human anger betrays your creation?

Disrupting both human and natural life with intent to generate fear.

May we see the seeds of your justice spark light into the darkness of human injustice.

May we see seeds of compassion spark, when human compassion has been placed aside.

May we be the spark of light to your design here on earth.

May we be the light to push aside fear.

May we receive your strength to fight for your Justice, for your compassion.

May we receive the strength to prioritize your vision of love over human power.

Prayer for Christmas

You vulnerably came to us as a child, knowing you would be hurt.
You came to us without a home.
You came to us in love.
May we help light the world with your hope.
May we always help those in need.
May we stay humble and share your love.

Prayer for communion

We thank you Creator, for becoming flesh like us.

We thank you Jesus, for suffering physically like us.

We are broken, just as your body was.

We thank you Creator, for your grace.

We thank you Creator, for inviting us to eat at your table, though our worthiness is lacking.

May we remember that you became our servant, and washed our feet.

May we remember to serve our community.

May we remember your physical body was broken.

May we remember your blood was shed and soaked by the Earth.

Jesus, you lived among us, you died among us.

God of mercy, your love is beyond understanding.

Prayer for Fall

Creator of all, You created beautiful fall leaves.

They brighten, shine, and fall.

They blanket the ground and keep it warm.

They degrade to nourish the earth for new growth and new life.

May my life be a colorful light to the world.

May my life blanket and cover your creation and all those that are around me and need comfort and protection.

May my life nourish your world in a way that brings new life and ideas to the world.

Mourn

Is it OK to mourn?

To mourn when we have placed faith in the wrong place?
Forgive us Lord, when our faith is placed in anything other than you.

Is it OK to mourn?

To mourn for those whose fear of being separated from their family is real.

Is it OK to mourn?

For those whose fear of losing their freedom is real.

Is it OK to mourn?

For those whose fear of losing their home is real?

Is it OK to mourn

For those whose fear of losing their planet is real?

Is it OK to mourn?

For those whose fear has blinded them to truth?

Let us remember the power you have given us for change.
Let us remember how to continue to transform this world into a world of love, with justice for all.

Let us remember how to fight for Justice.

Let us remember how to love.

Let us find new ways to fight injustice.

Let us find new ways to spread the message of love.

Let us find new ways to care for the nature that supports us.

Help us to find new ways to open the eyes of the blind.

May your realm be implemented on Earth as it is in Heaven.

Before your throne

Lord Almighty God.

We know you never leave our side and always listen when we talk to you.

We ask that you reach deep inside each of us and bring forth before your throne our needs, our fears, our praise.

Respond to us with your counsel, your peace, your healing, and power.

Poems

Do not beat yourself up

When you are weak,
When you are sad,
When you are depressed,
When you are angry,
When you are confused,
Do not beat yourself up.

True Joy comes from God,
Deep understanding comes from God,
Full Comfort comes from God,
Real Peace is a gift from God,
Inner strength a blessing of God,
Do not beat yourself up.

Yes we can do God's work toward Justice,
Yes we can help by sharing God's Love,
Yes we can be a tool of God's mercy,
Yes we can do more,
Do not beat yourself up.

Take Responsibility,
You may be defeated,
You may fail,
God will not fail,
Do not beat yourself up.

Trust,
Hope,
Love,
Faith,
These are from somewhere far deeper than ourselves,
Do not beat yourself up.

Forgive yourself,
Forgive others,
For God has already forgiven you,
Show Mercy,
Live with Love,
Work for Justice.

Rebuild

What to do with anger ?
What to do with shame ?
What to do about injustice ?
What to do with sorrow ?

Hope for change,
Hope for Justice,
Hope for Peace,
View with Love.

What action will bring Justice ?
What action will bring Comfort ?
What action will bring Peace ?
What action will bring Love ?

Let us find the answers to these questions.
Let us work to change the broken systems.
For a better world for all people.
Let us do this out of Love.
Let us all rise to a better society.
Lets us rise to a better self.

Together, we can change,
Together, we can build equity,
Together means all, no exclusions.
Individually we will fail, yet individually we will make an impact,
To change what is broken, what is unjust.
Rise up together to usher in a new Society,
The present is broken, the future is Open.

Let us build anew.
May God hear our cry, and strengthen us as we rebuild a world based on Justice, and a Love that brings Peace to all people.

New life

After night, morning comes.

After the darkness, there is light.

After a flower dies, there is a new seed.

Like a flower, even if we wither, we have within us a seed for new life.

Morning comes.

Seeds within us bring new life.

Love

The pain is real!
God is real!
Fear is real!
God is real!
Sorrow is real!
God is real!
Loss is real!
God is real!
We are not alone, for God is with us.
We are not alone, for we have neighbors here and across the world.
Our fears, our sorrows, our loss our pain ties us together.
God's love binds us together.
Share your love with someone today.

Cry

When is it time to cry ?
People are dying.
People are mourning.
Healthcare workers are putting their lives in danger.
Janitors are putting their lives at risk.
As we continue to be overwhelmed by loss and
the weight of the pain of those around us.
Let us remember crying for others
is part of our humanity.
May it comfort you knowing your emotions is
part of how we know we are able to love, and one
of the ways we are made in God's image.

Guns under God ?

Oh Nation under God,
Why praise the AR-15 ?
Why praise the automatic gun ?
Does everyone need a gun ?
Where is your trust in God the protector ?
Is the freedom to buy a gun worth more than the freedom of your children to live ?
Shall the guns run free and the children study in bunkers ?

Oh Nation under God,

When will you pound your guns into plowshare's ?

When will you trust God to protect you and not your own weapons ?

Oh Nation under God,

When will you give up your freedom of purchase for the freedom of your children to live ?

Oh Nation under God,

Stop your praise of the AR-15.

Stop your praise of your own power.

Your children are dying your churches and synagogues are under fire.

Oh Nation under God,

Close down your temples to riffles.

Close down your associations of death.

Close down your gun factories.

Chose the life of your children.

Chose the life of your citizens in the marketplace.

Oh Nation under God,
Turn your trust back to God.
Turn your guns into plowshares.
Turn your AR into AgRiculture.
Agriculture to feed the hungry.
The hungry for Peace.
The hungry for Justice.
The hungry for safety.
The hungry for food.

Oh Nation under God!

Be Light

Remember when Darkness is around us our light is more visible no mater how small.

Keep being light with your love and kindness.

Can you see?

Oh can you see?
How greed builds cruelty?
To feed greed you need to take.
Take from the poor.
Take from the sick.
Take from the disfranchised.
Take from the overworked.

Oh can you see?
How to hide greed with cruelty?
Disappear the mother and brother.
Disappear the sisters and fathers.
Question the truth tellers.
Scare the unenlightened.
Question the just.
Overwork the servant.
Confuse, and take more.

Oh can you see?
How to fight greed and cruelty?
Love the neighbor and the stranger.
Feed the poor.
Care for the sick.
Challenge injustice.
Expose lies and untruths.

Oh can you see?
A society of caring.
A society of sharing.
A society where you are the positive charge.
Be brave be free.
Light society with love.
Light and expose greed and cruelty.

To Be or not to Bee

When you share love with the world.

When you do a kindness for a neighbor.

When you share a smile with a stranger.

When you support someone in need .

You may feel you are like an insect in your contribution,

Yet some Insects make an immense contribution to the survival of humanity.

You are an immense contribution to humanity.

When you share love,

When you support anyone in need,

When you are a light to someone .

Just as insects can be beautiful to some, you are beautiful to me, to others, to God, when you pollinate the world with Love, one kindness at a time.

God is with you

When you feel sorrow from those around you.
When you sense your fear or the fear of others .

God is there!

Pray for strength.
Pray for wisdom.

Strength to fight injustice.
Wisdom to understand how you can help.
Wisdom to see where to shine your light.

God will not abandon us, no matter how badly humans treat God's creation, both human and nature.

God is there!

Defeat No!

Defeat No!
Stand back up!
Defeat No!
Stand back up!
Defeat No!
Wipe away your tears.
Defeat No!
Resist!
Defeat No!
Stand up for Justice,
Defeat No!
Stand up for your neighbor,

Defeat No!
Shine your light brighter,
Defeat No!
Stand back up,
Defeat No!
Stand up for the poor,
Defeat No!
Stand up for the stranger,
Defeat No!
Stand up for the weak,
Defeat No!
Stand up for those without a voice,
Defeat No!
Stand up against violence,
Defeat No!
Stand up against evil,
Defeat No!
Stand up for Love.

Meditation

As God breathed life into you;
Breathe in: God Loves me,
Breathe out: God loves the world,
Breathe in: God's love in,
Breathe out: Gods love shared.
Repeat as needed.
God has breathed life into you.
Breathe out Gods love to the world

List of Photographs

www.ingramcontent.com/pod-product-compliance
Lightning Source LLC
LaVergne TN
LVHW070222110826
845147LV00003B/625

* 9 7 9 8 9 9 5 6 8 1 1 3 7 *